Ketamine

QUARANTINE

CONFESSIONS

2

x

the fun of
(sober) volume
1

BRODY McVITTIE

WARNING
(-in lieu of a preface)

Never really one
for semblance of structure
or perfect plot

and so
apologies;

while Quarantine Confessions 1
(--on sale now)

had a narrative more
representative of what you might
commonly find

in books like these

--this one,
Quarantine Confessions 2
follows the completely non-
sensical

non-direction

of this fucking Pandemic

no end in sight

and more exhausting than
it has any right to be.

PART ONE

Poems for Being Sad.
(In a Global Pandemic.)

JUNE.
(The second June since this
whole mess started.)

171 million infected and
3.7 million killed

and I swore I wouldn't obsess
about numbers anymore

but I also swore I wouldn't
obsess about you

and we both know my ability
to be honest

pales in comparison to my
ability to both write and
obsess,

and so here I am

doing my part to ensure
you're filled with stats and
longings.

FUCK PAGE NUMBERS,
THIS IS ONE OF THOSE
CONVENTION BE DAMNED
PUT-THE-TENDER-SENSIBILITIES-TO-BED
PAGE TURNERS

SO
DOG EAR THE ONES ABOUT YOU AND
WONDER WHAT I WAS THINKING

THE FIRST TIME I READ IT BACK AND TOO

AND THEN WONDER WHAT YOU'LL BE THINKING
THE FIRST TIME I READ IT TO YOU.

*some of this is about you
some of this is about her
and
--as much as it kills you
one or two are about *her*

i'll leave it up to you
and the rest of the readership
to decipher semi-well-intentioned
meanings
behind words, mean and otherwise
that mean more to some
than ot**hers**.

Okay, so I haven't written
since the last booked wrapped,

(mid)
MARCH

and the madness supposed/not
really ended lockdowns wrought.

So here we are, and it's later
and the lockdown is gonna end
(FOR REAL THIS TIME!)

and I'm walking to the clinic
and for my very first poke,

and all I can think of

is you and

the mess losing you cost me and
the rest of the world.

So it's June
300 million doses, here

and it may be one, and it may be two
and admittedly I'm not great at
reading data

like I'm not great at reading signs
like the signs I should have read

the signs that read

DANGER

well before some fucking virus
stopped my world

the way you were dying to.

I've had it
with girls named after seasons

they last almost as long
as their collective namesakes;

and so, for Christ's sake
could I meet someone
with half the staying power

of fucking seven-seasons
You.

LOOK, I NEVER REALLY UNDERSTOOD THE
PHASES
BUT I'M TOLD TWO NEEDLES AND A COUPLE
TENDAYS

AND WE'RE OUT OF THIS MESS
THE WAY WE REALLY NEED TO BE

BECAUSE

OUR FAVORITE RESTAURANT CLOSED
AND I'LL NEVER SEE MY BARBER AGAIN

AND THE WORLD WE'RE INHERITING
DOESN'T LOOK LIKE THE WORLD WE PUT ON
PAUSE

AND SO PAUSES
CAN JOIN PHASES

ON MY LIST OF THE EVER-INCREASING
WORDS WE ARE NOT ALLOWED TO SAY.

TAMMY

according to her name tag.

is my injection specialist.

And it's not fun.
like Botox
or Heroin

but she's all I've got
and so it's Moderna
or Pfizer

and naps

so I can get back to
the comforts of
Heroin
and poems about you.

The needle goes in and

I suppose I'm supposed to feel
something

but

I'm as numb to the vaccine
coursing through my veins

as I am ambivalent to the
situation I find myself in

alone in self-imposed
apocalypse

and no one
to commiserate over
ice-cream and brain-frozen
semi-serious schemes.

The news tells me

I'm likely to grow a third eye

and I'm all for it,

perspective and wisdom and

the things third eyes bring

less concerned about side-effects than the ability to weaponize freedom

and go places other than the liquor stores

your absence

and this apocalypse

have left me infrequently frequenting.

My status

--according to my status card

tells me I'm eligible for the
second poke

significantly faster than
the non-status

status of the person beside me.

And I'll take it

despite the whispers that

individuals sharing my status
get fast-tracked for reasons

rhyming with schmexperimental

because the hopeless romantic
in me

appreciates the government-
issued

free heroin/whiskey/ketamine
of it all.

SHE TELLS ME I MIGHT BE A LITTLE
SORE,

TAMMY DOES

AND I JUST LOOK AT HER AND LAUGH

A POKE AND PANDEMIC SYRUP

HAS NOTHING ON

THE NEEDLES I USE

TO COPE WITH ISOLATION

AND

YOU.

2.9 billion vaccines
administered worldwide

and I'm one of them, now

thanks to Tammy and her

'you call that a needle'

needle

and I'm on the fast track for dose
two

and on the way home to make
horrible decisions

decidedly related to you.

SCARY HOURS ARE THE ONLY HOURS I KEEP.

in case I don't feel good

following the steps I take

in confidence and the semi-
promised assurances

we can have our world back;

on some of these pages

to remind you,

in case the poem on this page

is the last semi-good-faith
scribble

my scrambled mind can scribble.

(mid)
JUNE.
(And the delerious rants of a post first poked mind)

Call me Mr. Moderna

better in doses

decidedly smaller

so read these

a page or two at a time

any more

and I'll have you

laid out

feverish

and reading a little more into it

than you most assuredly should.

THE FEVER HITS

AND IT'S LESS VACCINE

AND MORE THE KETAMINE/WHISKEY I CHASE
IT WITH;

AND MY FREQUENT LAPSES
IN BOTH JUDGMENT AND MENTAL HEALTH

HAVE ME ERASING THE PROGRESS
I MAKE IN QUARANTINE CONFESSIONS VOLUME
ONE

LESS FUN

THAN THE MAL-INTENTIONED MACHINATIONS
OF THIS

THE FIRST SEQUEL BETTER THAN THE ONE
BEFORE.

you ask how long I'll love you
and it's forever
and at least all of the everydays within it
as long as we have
you'll remember the love
long after questions fade
and time takes
all of the everything-else it can have

love that's left
all that's left

and more than enough.

Fuck you,

I'll take

Old soul

over

No soul

any day of the week.

TOXIC YEAH

BUT IN A FUN WAY.

i care a lot less

about the money I'll never make

the cars I'll never drive

the places I'll never go;

I care a lot more

about the things i would have bought you

the backseat of the car i would have given
them to you in

Uber'd up around some island i only visit

in dreams i only always dream about you

I'd trade all six of my abs

and all forty of my (fucking
forty already)

years

for two and a half more with
you.

Like maybe we could make up
for

the two and a half we maybe
kinda wasted,

all rampaging insecurities

and the kind of mind-
blowing make up sex

rampaging insecurities
make worthwhile.

You're bad with scissors
and carefully crafted words.

You're worst on Wednesdays --
i guess getting over that particular hump
was always made harder by my fucking
selfish ability to just kind of be around.
So put down the pointy things
take the breath you were saving
for the yelling you're about to--
because that Wednesday night show is about
to start
and punching holes is better saved for the
plotlines.

STOP ME

IF YOU'VE HEARD THIS ONE

I'M NOT OVER IT.

write,

hope it resonates,

wait.

you know

and I know

this shit will hit different when
I'm dead

so waiting

is about as effective

as telling you to read this

and the rest

I've lost rest

hoping you'll care enough to read.

ALL SOLD OUT OF SELF PRESERVATION
AND THE SORT OF THING

THAT SHOULD PROBABLY PREVENT

THE NEXT PAGE

AND THE PAGES THAT FOLLOW.

Fuck you,

Have this one for free,

it's not like you'd pay for it

(the way you're gonna pay for it on every
single one of these pages)

anyways.

And anyways,

enjoy ;)

Keep all your

Red-State Desert Heat Baby-Factory

Indignations

Aimed squarely at

the Anybody-else you could almost get to

take you and those criminally blue eyes

back.

You're lucky I chose

POEMS NO ONE READS

over the (now, in hindsight

infinitely more profitable)

SONGS EVERYONE BOPS.

No machine to push this

None of the trendier ethnicities

or de jeur gender pronouns

just good old fashioned, cancel-worthy
rage

and disdain for the kind of heart that
could break

such an easily breakable heart.

Low-key Savage

since 21

and 21

(minus 1)

older now

means that while I still

love a good Bieber song,

I'm burdened by both

the beasts and beats

Mick and maybe Jon Bon wrote about

These Days

spent reminiscing about

those days.

JULY.
(And just in time for Jab Two.)

182 million infected and
3.9 million killed

and maybe I'm numb to the
numbers

but that first jab didn't kill
me

the way you and COVID seem to
want to,

and the alone you've both
left me to be

is about to close

the way we're about to
(hopefully)

open.

Almost a year off,

One corporate call in

And I'm ready for the world to

Shut the fuck down again.

REGRET IS A FUNNY THING.

LIKE RELIGION.

The older I get the more I realize

biology betrays

chemistry stays

like I should have loved science

A little maybe more than I did

A little less time admiring

A little more time investigating

Why I found you so irresistible too

Chalking it up

the way foolish boys do

to the dark of your hair

over the particles inside

the eyes I appreciated

at least as much as mine.

DON'T GO TO BED BROKEN

-FIRST/LATEST IN A LINE OF RULES
I'M INTENT ON BREAKING TONIGHT AND
EVERY OTHER.

I always required

a degree of patience

a modicum of pity

at least a rudimentary understanding of
circumstance

circumstance, my favorite four-letter
word

when it comes to

the humility you so bravely displayed

in the painfully short years worth of
encounters

that made it painfully obvious

dealing with me was a little more than

advertised on my cleaner surfaces.

So, to recap

CHEMISTRY > BIOLOGY

Math Science class couldn't teach me

half as good as you did.

I’m back at work and it’s working

wonders for an admittedly
shattered state of mind,

and I don’t

mind

being around people,

even if being around people

means being around their wildly
inaccurate opines on the reasons
why

their either jabbed or not jabbed

and while logic
and the need to get back to some
state of norm

dictates being back under the
oppression of corporate life

is necessary too,

I can’t help but wonder

If wildly inaccurate opines
are as part of the ‘new normal’

as faces hidden

the way intentions used to be.

I failed famous
like Grade 10 math
and there's a chance

IF YOURE READING THIS

I failed you, too
and so

IF YOURE READING THIS ITS
TOO LATE

like I should have dropped a mixtape,

and you should have skipped this story.

RUMINATIONS

MACHINATIONS

&

other big words

from a tiny mind.

To be fair,
I was writing about
my mental health

unhealth

about twenty before it was trendy

so I turn a phrase
like you turn a back

and I twist tongues, cool
you curl yours

and toes
in the sheets you twist and turn

twisting up schemes
to fix your mental

unhealthy

ability
to waste time missing

--more than my writing.

13 books

20 years

627 chapters

1345 poems

1, 307, 642 words

0 flowers.

(so give me those.)

*while I'm still living.
**pretty please.

still

&

stay

&

all of the words my eyes tell you.

DRIVE AWAY

PRETEND IT DOESN'T KILL YOU A
LITTLE BIT, TOO.

Days and days go by
and
the absence of you
lingers
in a way I wish your ghost would.

Hauntings metaphorical
and
not half the fun

of peering down half-lit halls
and
wondering what corner
you're handsomely hiding behind.

The hair you left
on hardwood floors

(*the hair I swore I'd never finish
cleaning up)

is conspicuously absent too

And so the days that pass
are cleaner;

but half the fun
of the hiding you and that damn
hair

used to haunt me

down hallways and the cracks
between floorboards.

Softer than

the cookies you used to bake

on Friday nights

better suited for baking.

The half-baked

writing I'm doing now

about as half-hearted

as the effort you put back into me

forever envious

of those goddamned cookies.

I've run out of

-creative expression
-good taste
-patience

And so maybe this

is the totality

of the little that's left;

Half-hearted musings

of the half you took

leaving me to the ramblings

I scribble on the pages

you maybe only care to read

Running, and in

decidedly opposite directions.

OKAY, YOU'RE RIGHT

KNOWING YOU'RE SOMEWHERE FUMING
ABOUT IT

WAS AT LEAST HALF THE REASON

I WROTE

THAT LAST LITTLE THING

I WROTE ABOUT YOU.

I turn to the whiskey
Because the world is still shut off

And although I've done my part
I'm told to wait until the malcontents do
theirs

And so

I turn to the whiskey
And it whispers to me
And in the talking

The "where have you beens"
Become "hey, remember her?" 's

And I'm back on the sauce
And I'm thinking

Maybe I'm The Sauce, too

And so I'm calling you
The way the liquid courage
And the rampant loneliness

Have me calling you

...And the rest of this book that follows

Follows my inability to deal with

The pick up or don't

You're most certainly about to.

Mr. Misgiving.

If there's 1 thing Rambo 2 taught me,

it's that burying my sadness

under peptide-accelerated tans and an aggressively ridiculous lack of body fat

is the best way to deal with

the PTSD of losing

You and the latest

of the losing things

me and my moderately unhealthy tan

are resigned to.

Really, it's your fault

For loving badly broken boys.

I went to the fridge
to grab
the last of the cookies you baked

I made the mistake of bringing my
notebook with me

five poems & one still open door later

I'm ten crumbs & half a lightbulb away
from

the exasperating existentialism that
comes

when the last of the cookies go

the way of fridge lightbulbs
and the pride it takes
to put down the pen
and pick up the phone
and thank you
at the very least
for the savory sweetness that lingers
knowing I'll never eat cookies again.

If you're looking for

emotionally stunted,
scared little boys

who puff their chests out trying
to be anything else,

You've come to the right place.

YOU GO IN THAT SPECIAL PLACE
LIKE MY DOG DABBER FROM WHEN I
WAS SIX

A PERFECT MEMORY

AND THE KIND OF PRESENT

THAT MAKES EVERY PULLING OF
THAT FIRST LEG

THROUGH THE PANTS I'M HOPING
WILL CARRY ME THROUGH THE DAY

JUST A LITTLE MORE PAINFUL

THAN STARTING ANOTHER DAY
HAS ANY RIGHT TO BE.

2 many million infected and
2 many million killed

and it's white noise to me
now
because it kinds feels like
I'm getting my world back
and while getting my world
back should maybe mean you

I'll that the reemergence of
the economy and a modicum of
normality in the interim

to be spent scheming schemes
on how to make their lack of
restrictions (relatively
speaking)

last longer than we had any
right to.

GET OVER IT

ALL OVER AGAIN.

I'm early, in terms of time wasted
waiting for that second poke,
Vaccine injection #2 coming faster
than half-believed promises
of days with indoor activities in them,
seeing people for the first time
in what has been a long time,

and the one person I can' t wait to see
is the one person who maybe meant it
when they said they never really want
to
see me

DELORES

according to her name tag.

is my injection specialist.

And it's not fun,
like Sodomy
or Heroin

but she's all I've got
and so it's Moderna .
again

and more naps

so I can get back to
the comforts of
Heroin
and poems about you.

The needle goes in and

I suppose I'm supposed to feel
something this time

and

maybe I'm a little less numb to the
vaccine
coursing through my veins

a little less alone in self-
imposed
apocalypse

knowing maybe no one
to commiserate over
ice-cream and brain-frozen
semi-serious schemes

is as temporary
as the supposed pain from this
supposed last needle.

I've got friends

(--believe it or not)

that are violently anti-vax

and while part of me wants to support
the likely misbegotten concept of personal
freedom

the part of me that wants
you and the ability to see you

across tables and in decidedly public
places

quietly hopes

they'll join me and the rest of the so-
called 'sheep'

in doing our part to keep 2020
in the past where it fucking should be.

STUFF CAN OPEN

IT SAYS ON THE NEWS

AND SO I'M HOPING

IN THE OPENING

YOU TAKE MY AGGRESSIVELY OPEN

INVITATION

TO INVITE YOURSELF

INTO MY SWEAR-IT'S-DIFFERENT-THIS-TIME

WORLD

THE ONE I HOPE
A CONVENIENTLY TIMED GLOBAL CRISIS

LEFT YOU ROSE-COLORED IN THE
REMEMBERING.

PART TWO.

Poems for Becoming Infatuated.
(In a Global Pandemic.)

August.
(and not just everything after.)

198 million infected and
4.2 million killed

and summer has me pretending
any of that is okay,

because I'm allowed to go
places for the first time in
tiny forevers

but why would I want to,
isolation and outright
apathy fighting summer sun
outside,

outside allegedly 'okay'
again.

Passports
to go anywhere

but

there's nowhere to go

now
where

would I be
without isolations
self-imposed or otherwise;

and so the restaurants & bars
can stay open

the bars I stay behind
caged in a mind I made up

long before passports
and external circumstances.

People are losing
jobs & sanity
and you can feel it on the
streets

fender bendings & raised
voices

reserved for forums
where both reservations &
decorum

demand anything but

but the faith I have
in the humanity I lost
tells me we'll be okay

and I'm not,
but hey

--they can't all be about me
the way they're all about
you.

Manifested

Misery

&

Malintent

'Someday'

is a trigger.

I ALMOST GAVE UP
ON SOME
'WHY NOT GIVE UP'
SHIT;

THE WHISKEY WHISPERED
REMINDERS THAT

OF ALL THE THINGS
I'M REALLY JUST NOT
I'M REALLY JUST NOT
THE ONE TO QUIT

THE WAY YOU AND MY SOBRIETY
COULDN'T WAIT TO.

I take my coffee

the way you took

my rational ability

to just kind of get by

and I am,
you know,

getting by
and barely

wanting to less

because you left me
to stronger coffee

and the kind I have to
make my own damn self.

It's Orwellian,
this dystopia we find ourselves
in,

or it's not
1984

nothing to you
save one admittedly really good
Taylor Swift album

some thirteen years
before you came around

and some thirteen months
since this dystopia

(maybe)
weighed on you enough

to make you
and your pop-informed decisions

worthy of memory holes

and

the kind you punched clear
through me

totalitarian

in your ability

to take a globally bad situation

and

somehow make it worse.

I'm sick of writing
about pandemics and the pain that
comes with it

as you are,
reading too many pages like this one

desperately lonesome

and desperately writing
in the hopes

that hope
is enough

to do something about
the latest of things

I'm sick of having no control over.

Regret?

Volumes worth,

the latest & last

you hold in the hands

I'd much rather

hold me.

Unquestionably Underrated

&

Appropriately Unconscionable.

I SWORE I WAS DONE

QUARANTINE CONFESSIONS 1

BUT YOU LEFT

ME TO FOURTH WAVES

AND WAVING GOODBYE

OUT WINDOWS

OTHERSIDE OF THE WALLS

THE GOVERNMENT PREFERS I HIDE
BEHIND.

SO

QUARANTINE CONFESSIONS 2

AND

FUCK YOU.

Vaxx

or

No Vaxx

you're all assholes

to me.

The ring I didn't
wasn't the ring I wouldn't
you just assumed
the way I did,
believing you
when you told me
you didn't/wouldn't.

So lie
the way you did,
wonder why I shouldn't.

I almost gave up
on some
"why not give up"
shit;

the whiskey whispered
reminders that

of all the things
I'm really just not

I'm really just not

the one to quit

the way you and my sobriety
couldn't wait to.

Your eyes
don't make sense
&
your ass
is the one-of-a-kind

those prescription-weak glasses

only reflect

the subtleties my gaze
clearly lacks

looking back at you
&
those eyes
&
that ass
&

wondering why I ever bothered to
write about anything else.

I'm back at the liquor store
and it's weird because we're
allowed to go places now,

and while I'm actually kind of
happy to see

somewhat normal people join me in
the quest to medicate themselves,

I can't help but feel

things being open

is as now-strange

as this being decidedly-not

used to be.

You're looking at me,

all eyes-that-don't-make-sense

and I can't

make sense of the reasons you're
choosing to fix a gaze better suited

(literally) any-elsewhere

at me and my not-even-broken-toy
cute

suffering personage.

I'll take it,

as Hail Mary salvations go,

you and those eyes

&

that ass

suited to saving

decidedly more

than the last sip of whiskey

we're suddnenly sharing

atop couches previously suited

for isolations and abject sadness.

September.

218 million infected and
4.5 million killed and

...fuck this.

Fuck it

I'm taking a month off
because things are open and
maybe not for long

but this month
writing about feelings means
feeling them

and the sunshine in the world-
there-still-is outside

means I'd rather be out there

and I'd rather just not.

I took September off

and so sorry that chapter sucked

I promise to make it up to you

the way all the words

in all the books

kinda just couldn't.

Gobtobler.

234 million infected and
4.8 million killed

and it's still kinda summer
outside and summer has a way
of fooling us into thinking
it's okay

and it's really still kinda
anything but

okay

and here's really fucking
hoping this coming fall

is the last fall

we fall for all of this.

Gobtobler

is what we called it

when nicknaming months
made months the kind of
bearable

they're really just not.

Gobtobler

just the month you moved in
the first & latest

of months both too long
and not the fun they

used to/should be.

The mall is filled
with masked up zombies

shambling around stores
hopelessly filled with sanitizers

in hopes that emasciated, zombie
fingers

finger fondling every piece of
clothing

strewn atop forgot-how-to-stock
shelves

does enough in the way of
combating inevitable fourth waves

to make shopping for This Fall's

Must Have Top!

anything other than

the outright masturbatory exercise
in futility

returning to shopping in malls
ever again

already is.

Every post-apocalyptic movie on
Netflix, ever

told us this was coming

In lieu of blindly leaping
into the oblivion of inevitability,

I'm happy the couch I watched this
all coming from

was the couch I shared with you.

Passports

aren't just tickets to exotic places now

and the restrictions

we're admittedly used to be restricted to

are as commonplace as the distrust
they tend to produce

but I'll produce mine,
this passport decidedly less fun

than the aforementioned kind

if it means I can access
places to purchase produce

and sink further into a beautifully
foolish dream

that this isn't reality and the rest of

my somber little semi-life.

AMIDST

AN EVER INCREASING

SERIES OF

INCREASINGLY SERIOUS

RESTRICTIONS AND REGULATIONS

YOU'RE

THE ONE THING

THAT MAKES THE REST OF

THESE ENTIRELY NONSENSICAL

EVERYTHINGS

MAKE SOMETHING SEMI CLOSE

TO SENSE.

You know it's getting bad

when Tammy, my injection
specialist

and

Delores, my injection specialist

are two of the most important-
significant characters

in this little book;

guess I don't get out as much as I
maybe used to

and guess I'm maybe used to
a world where met-you-once
injection specialists

are among the more significant
interactions

a man can make
in the course of a really shitty
half-year.

I'm in the throes
of self-imposed
makeshift miseries
and the woes
that inevitably come
with mid-life make-believes

when here you come,
perpetual high-pony
and the kind of
'married' that makes
chasing
worth something
stronger than whiskey I chase
to muster the strength to.

Black Ink
White Paper

because the colors ran
out of my worldview
and American spelling
and just Grey

all that's left
right or not

no matter what spellchecks
or concerned parents
say

all I'm left with
is all You left.

Here's to Skullduggery

&

Sadness.

I'm thinking about the walks
And the talks that inevitably came with

(--and not just because that shit rhymes)

You know I was always a better poet than that

But not enough of one
To scare you into staying

Like fear of the (also inevitable) Tell-All

We both knew I'd eventually have to publish

Told you like the talks on those walks

That talking you into sticking around

Wasn't something you're thinking back on

And thinking maybe you should have

YOU LOOK AT ME
WITH EYES THAT DON'T MAKE SENSE
AND
MAYBE SHOULDN'T

LOOKING AT ME
IS PRECURSOR TO THE KNOWING ME
THAT GNAWS AT YOU
LONG AFTER LINGERING LOOKS
FADE INTO ABJECT INDIGNATION

Call me

after you read this

i'll color all the commentary

you pretend you don't comprehend.

For what it's worth
I read all the great books
to make a great man

The Prince
couldn't fix me
&
Thoughts or Meditations
didn't land the way Marcus maybe hoped
&
while
The 120 Days of Sodom
was fun, the Marquis came closest
but couldn't

save

one scared little boy
from deep rooted feelings of

feeling not so great.

"I'M GETTING RID OF THE PARTS I WROTE
WHEN I WAS DRUNK"

MEANS

QUARANTINE CONFESSIONS 2

IS

2 PAGES

&

ONLY

&

1 OF THOSE

IS THE TITLE PAGE.

It's
National Boyfriend Day

because that's a thing
&
the thing of it is

I used to be boyfriend
material
&
now
the nation that reads this

is really thankful I'm not

small town boy

medium town ambitions

and while I didn't / have not

conquered the world
we find ourselves in

13 books and
the groupies that follow

distract me from
the more glaring of failures

I find myself

familiarly failing.

It rains

a little much for my liking

fall falling a little fast

for my liking

&

temperment suitings alone,

I'd rather leaves take time in their
collective leavings,

&

me to

the mirth that comes

with rapidly falling rains

&

rapidly turning leaves.

FOR
A GUY WHO SPENT
HIS BEST YEARS
PUTTING TRUTHS TO PAPER

THE TRUTH IS
YOURS IS THE ONE STORY
I'D LIKE TO KEEP
ALL TO MYSELF.

YOU'RE ALL
HIGH PONY
HIGH SOCKS
AND THE EFFECT ON ME
IS AFFECTING MY RELATIVELY SELFISH
ABILITY TO BE WALLOWING IN MISERY

THE LENGTH OF THOSE LEGS
AND THE HEIGHT OF YOUR HAIR
HAS ME COMMITTING BAD IDEAS TO PAPER
AND RELEGATING BAD INTENTIONS
TO THE DARK PLACES
PREVIOUSLY FILLED WITH
WHAT HAS TURNED OUT TO BE
ATTRACTIVE SELF-DESTRUCTIVNESS

SELF-DESTRUCTIVENESS

I'M HAPPY TO SHARE WITH YOU

AND THOSE RIDICULOUSLY

LONG LEGS.

Go on,

tell me I'm no good

I'm only on Page 125

of the 200 I need

to sell this book &

save this soul &

seal this damn

dam &

patch this hole

YOU'LL HAVE TO EXCUSE ME

BUT YOU AND THOSE

DON'T MAKE ANY KIND OF SENSE EYES

HAVE LEFT ME OUT OF THE KIND OF WORDS

I NORMALLY RESERVE

TO OUTLINE

THE MISTAKES

YOU'RE ABOUT TO MAKE.

Equal parts

scared little boy

&

tortured artist

&

semi-well-intentioned

interested party.

You still hurt more
than stubbed toes & skinned
knees

bad reviews & unrecognized
greatness

so congrats

you own the place
the pieces go to hide

bruised & bloodied & somehow
still

waiting for you to pick them up

& discard them all over again.

HAD THE LAST OF
THE LAST BATCH OF COOKIES
YOU BAKED BEFORE
YOU SAID GOODBYE.

AND, TO BE HONEST, THEY WERE THE KIND OF
BITTER

MY METAPHORICALLY INCLINED MIND MUST
SAY

SAYING GOODBYE TOOK THE SWEET
OUT OF THAT PARTICULAR BRAND
OF PARTICULARLY SUGARY TREAT

AND SO THE COOKIES ARE GONE

TOO

AND I'M LEFT TO CLEAN UP
THE CRUMBS OF YOU.

I'm good with words
but not good enough
to keep Red-haired her
or blonde-haired her
(or blonde-haired her)
or black-haired her
(and that one, in particular and
particularly hurt)

So forgive me
if Brown-haired You
is met with cautionary tales
and the kind of trepidation
that prefers you are kind,

in your judgements of me
and
the words misspelled on purpose
and
in efforts to keep you.

THAT GYPSY TOLD ME

YEAH, I'M GOOD AND CURSED

AND FUCKING GLOBAL PANDEMICS ASIDE

MY LUCK'S BEEN PRETTY GOOD

IF YOU COUNT

LOSING THE LATEST

IN A LAUNDRY LIST OF

ADMITTEDLY EPIC LOSSES

I'VE BEEN LOSING SINCE

THAT FIGHT WITH JOHNNY REIMER

MY KEYS

YOU.

Big fan of

your eyes & that ass &

the things about you that
don't make sense

eyes & ass aside

things like the way you
bother with me

the way

the way I am doesn't seem to
bother you

the way it so clearly
bothered

every-all of the rest of
them

without those eyes & that
ass

the way they all
unfortunately are

also without me

your biggest, latest fan

& of the way you won't leave

the way they couldn't wait
to.

I'm on a date

and, aside from the oddities
associated

with showing two pieces of
government issued ID

and

two pdf documents
documenting my double dose

the rest of this,

first date Friday

is about as close to normal

as an emotionally destroyed

semi-talented
documentarian/writer can hope for;

and

so it's You

and

those eyes

and

that ass

and

this,

our first-last
semi-desperate attempt

at some fleeting form
of good-intentioned normalcy.

The line at the grocery store
is playing tricks on me
like we're almost out of this
mess we collectively find
ourselves in,

like there's light at the end
of this maybe-never-ending
checkout line,

hope for the lost souls like
me
and Hungry-Man dinner Fred,

in line & equally

& equally in this mess

& this line

& judging by the look on his
Hungry-Man face,

about the only guy in this
mess

& this line

maybe more miserable than me.

No marriage.

No kids.

No hope.

...right?

Blame Covid
for the rampant
pining these 139 pages or so
produce.
and I shop for my own now
masked up and hiding
the emotions I reserve
for grocery shopping
and writing
the really sad shit I write
because I have to
(fucking grocery shop.)

NO
SUCH
ANIMAL
IN
THE
WILD.

Sitting across tables

and over what might be really fucking good
salmon

and the i can't tell is less because i'm not
eating

and more because it's been seven years

since i've sat across tables

and stared into eyes

that burned for seven

with the kind of

'fuck you'

that swore i'd never have the opportunity

to sit across tables again.

I really don't remember
my dog Dabber

but I'm relatively sure
I wrote about her
more than once,

so you're in good company,

poem #142,

and

likely not the last
I'll write in order to

Remember

All of the things I should probably
forget about you.

Here's a deep cut

--I'm that oiled-up guy
playing saxophone on the
beach at the beginning of
'LOST BOYS'

little out of place,
but makes sense in the grand
scheme of things,

all "fuck it, it's a movie
about vampires anyways."

TO BE FAIR,

I'M NOT EVEN SURE SPEED DIAL IS A THING ANYMORE

BUT IF YOU ONLY TAKE ONE THING FROM

THIS ADMITTEDLY EXHAUSTING, SELF-INDULGENT HAIL MARY FOR MENTAL HEALTH

--YOU'RE FIRMLY PRESET #1

If this pandemic
proves the death of me

let my cost-effective
tiny tombstone read

HERE LIES ______

HE BROKE EVERYTHING HE EVER
TOUCHED

& HE YEARNED FOR THINGS HE NEVER
COULD

HE NEVER REALLY SOLD A BOOK
OR CLIMBED A MOUNTAIN

BUT HE SURE LIKED YOU A LOT.

It's late and you're tired
and I'm tired too

so I'll keep this one brief
and talk less about you.

Ever wonder how you end up with
Tupperware?

Like maybe mine came from

Her

or

Her

or

Her

or

Her

or

Her

or

Her

or

her

or

Her;

Red lids

I know I'd never buy

Never match the clear plastic bowls

one of you was so clearly fond of

and it accumulates

in your collective wakes;

Red lid reminders

that you were here

once

and, apparently, long enough

to move in Tupperware.

so
apparently
getting sick
from jab one or jab two
is something
some people do

blame the cocaine or the
whiskey
or the cocaine and the
whiskey
for the way my body
eagerly accepts
even the most dubious of
doses

so
bring on the booster
because I'm here for it

microdosing more than the
psyllicibin the lockdown
has me experimenting with

in light of other
medically beneficial (?)
medicines coursing through

already poisoned veins.

You come around
about as often as Adele albums

five years removed and maybe past due
because I've been needing and needy
neatly folding not easily contained
memories of the things you did
and the things you do
and continue to

so it's
water under the bridge
or it's not

my memories are as fuzzy
as the pictures we took
way back when
iPhone cameras were forgiving
the way you're maybe not so much.

pain comma plenty.

THE WAY MY MIND WORKS
DOESN'T WORK

BUT YOU DON'T SEEM TO MIND
AND SO HERE'S TO BOOK 13
OF MODERATELY MEDICATED MUSINGS

AS TO THE NOT-SO-SUBTLE WAYS
I INTEND TO WIN YOU BACK.

PART THREE.

Poems for Not Falling Apart.
(In a Global Pandemic.)

I don't see the parallels
because parallels are for
parking

and the past, recent
regurgitates reasons

you and you, plural
left for greener pastures

amidst claims it wasn't me

when the parking indicators
indicate

it sure as fuck was.

I filled a notebook
and three years for this

so, excuse me if the
memories that come back
come back hard

maybe they'll last longer
than global pandemics
and this stint
wherever you ran off to
runs to

but in the meantime
you can have this,
the contents of a notebook
and three good years

Hope it's enough
to keep you warm
in the years to come

the years I'm gone
and you're left
with the memories my
notebook

makes you remember

everytime you face the
words

facing back at you.

GHOST MEDICINE

FOR MEDICATING THE MORE ABSTRACT
OF YOUR FREQUENT COMINGS
AND TIRED GOINGS.

You're distractingly pretty
as pretty distractions go

and I am

going

to spend the rest of
the less pretty words
I typically paint with

painting praises
better heaped upon you.

APOLOGIES

IF DATING ME

WAS SPENDING COMPANY

WITH THE GHOSTS OF THEM

THEY RARELY REST

AND WHISPER THE LESS WELL-INTENTIONED

OF ALREADY ADMITTEDLY SEMI-WELL-
INENTIONED

WORDS I WHISPERED

NO LESS LOUDLY

IN AND AMONGST

THE WHISPERED WORDS

THAT DROVE YOU IN DIRECTIONS

THAT WILL ONE DAY

LEAVE YOU

(LIKE YOU LEFT ME)

JUST A GHOST

IN MY HEAD

AND A LITTLE LESS

NO BETTER THAN THE REST OF THEM.

I miss

Pizza Hut's lunchtime buffet
a TV show called Banshee
and
my slightly-wasted thirties

I barely remember
my dog Dabber
and
the way the world worked
when masks were just on Halloween

but
one thing I don't miss
and sure as fuck remember

is the way you looked at me
the very first time
you knew you were in love
and
the way I thought
my days of writing sad books were done

turns out I was wrong

and so good luck with
the rest of your already-better life

I'll be here
barely remembering
and writing

really sad books
about why
it's better to forget.

Write volumes
so I don't speak them

perceived cowardice in
person

betrays avarice behind
eyes
spent scanning pages

for the right words to
write

all the volumes it will
inevitably take

to make this up to you.

REST

IS
A

FOUR-LETTER WORD

&
REALLY

AND

I'M JUST

REALLY, REALLY SAD
IT DIDN'T WORK OUT

&
THE REST THAT
COMES MEANS I'LL
GET NONE

BECAUSE

REST

IS
A
FOUR-LETTER WORD

&
REALLY.

LOVE

IS
A

FOUR-LETTER WORD

TOO

&

UNFORTUNATELY.

There's hope in those legs
to say nothing of those eyes
and that ass

hope in the way
there's been anything but
since the last set of legs
to box my ears

boxed my ears
more than metaphorically

so wrap those lengthy legs
around me and more than metaphorically
because I'm here for it

you

and the emotional entanglements
we make in the tangling.

you seem to have

an ability to take over

the totality of my thought
process

I mean, I used to reserve some
for
professionally necessary misery
and
the abject morbidity that comes
with creativity like mine

--and now it's pretty much you.

BADLY BROKEN BOYS DO IT BETTER.

YOU
SAY THAT ADULT LIFE MAKES IT HARDER

AND I TELL YOU IT'S THE WORST
AND I WOULD SAY FOR THE BEST
BUT I'M SELFISH AND LIFE IS SHORT

SO SEEING YOU STAYS A PRIORITY

RIGHT UP THERE WITH THE SELF-IMPOSED
MISERY
IT TAKES TO WRITE THE KIND OF NOT-KIND
WORDS I WRITE

AND RIGHT UP THERE WITH THE LIES I TELL
MYSELF AND TO ASSURE ME I'M THE KIND OF
CLEVER IT TAKES

TO COME UP WITH A WAY AROUND
THE SELF-IMPOSED WALLS
YOU'RE SO POORLY IMPOSING.

these talks go best
when it’s impossibly late
&
impossible.

StAY

because I still need Jesus & a pretty big
bath

but the sins I wash away

aren't half the story of the ones that
StAY

the way your head tells you
you really, really shouldn't

but
that pull
in the pit of your tiny little stomach

tells you
you really, really should.

HONESTLY

...IS THIS SHIT AS EXHAUSTING TO YOU IN THE READING

AS IT WAS TO ME IN THE WRITING?

Write for days
talk for hours
because the time it takes
to mend the wounds
I'm so hell-bent on wounding
means I need more than just the minutes
it took to fool you
to talk myself out of
the months of messes
you and those fat little lips
are moving to convince me
time
is something we have anywhere close
to enough of.

FIRST-TEAM
ALL ENERGY

I GET THE FEELING
THIS IS THE ONE THAT WILL BLOW UP
AFTER I'M DEAD

LIKE THEY'LL SAY

"THAT @brodydrew COULDN'T HOLD A DAMN
RELATIONSHIP"

"OR MAKE ANYTHING OF HIMSELF WHEN HE
WAS HERE"

"BUT FUCK, COULD THAT HANDSOME DEVIL
TURN A PHRASE AND TWIST A TONGUE
SILVER AND OTHERWISE"

WINDING WORDS AND CHURNING
FEELINGS IN PLACES
YOU ONLY FEEL
WHEN THE PERSON RESPONSIBLE FOR THE
STORM

IS DEAD AND GONE AND

APPRECIATED LIKE THE SUN

AFTER SAID STORMING.

STILL

colder than your step-
father

when it comes to this
writing shit

and

daddy issues aside

I'll play roles
assigned only to places
your better judgment
goes to hide.

OF ALL THE EMOTIONS I COULD
INSTILL

I'LL TAKE "TERRIFIED"

HAPPY TO INSTILL EMOTIONS,
STRONG

OVER THE APATHY YOU SO
CLEARLY SAVE

FOR THE ONES YOU MAYBE
MEAN IT

WHEN YOU SAY

"love"

HERE'S TO HARSH FADES
&
HEAD SCARS.

SACCHARINE SADNESS

SWEET ENOUGH FOR YOUR MORNING COFFEE.

She says
“I have the most to lose”
and I’m like
“all due respect, it’s
mind
clothes
aside
you’re oh-so-safe with me.”

OF ALL THE THINGS
I'M OUT TO DO TO YOU,

"HURT"

ISN'T ONE OF THEM.

NOT TO PUSH THE BOUNDARIES

JUST KNOW YOU CAN'T MOVE THE GOALPOSTS FAR ENOUGH TO BE OUT OF BOUNDS.

lionize me

/

idolize you.

AROUND HERE

GOBTOBLER 25TH

IS THE DAY THIS ALL OFFICIALLY ENDS,

WHILE MASKS MIGHT BE AROUND UNTIL MARCH

THE END OF GOBTOBLER

SEES THE END OF THE RESTRICTIONS WE'VE BEEN OH-SO-RESTRICTED TO;

AND WHILE
GOBTOBLER
IS A PARTICULARLY SPOOKY SEASON--

--IT NOW HAS REASONS
OTHER THAN

THE GHOSTS OF
GOBTOBLER
PAST

TO CELEBRATE THE END

OF FEELINGS THAT FALL
LONGER THAN LINGERINGS

OF OVERSTAYED SICKNESS.

November

November

--can fuck right off

Gobtobler always spooky-long

and

lingering

like the ghost

you up and turned into.

November

for real this time

winter is coming

and

for any hope

I had prior to your goings

There's a formula for all of this;

meet her/love her/let her break you

let the pieces she leaves

leave you

set the scene amongst the horrors of
horribly oppressive globally-relatable
situations...
...fill this page, and the pages that
follow
with the kind of uncompromising rage
the pieces leave in their leaving,
too.
Or '2' because this is the sequel, latest
in a series of lamentations
directly related to the myriad reasons
why.

iT's aMazIng to mE

hoW the seconD parT of ThIS
comes eAsier

thaN the firsT

like writing sad shit about
the people you miss really
tries to make you miss the
people who could keep the
sadness somewhere else.

November and the inevitable arrival of
flu season

Practically guarantees Quarantine
Confessions 3

like vaccinations comma billions

can keep the restrictions that constrict

us

the away we've all prayed/waited for

for at least as long as I've been putting

sad shit to paper,

way too

and longing for a flu season that is a

flu season and just.

I realize I'm running out of road

patience you have for writing like this
wearing as thin as the fabric of the
workout pants I prefer you
workout in
but(t) if you bear (bare) with me, I promise
more than immature ramblings designed
to fake a depth
you've seen through since
I noticed how good you really do look
in those thin fabric workout pants.

WE REALLY DO NEED
TO STOP FOR A SECOND
AND FIGURE OUT
THOSE FUCKING EYES

...THEY DON'T MAKE SENSE
AND I'M LOSING MINE
AND MORE THAN THE ONE
THAT CAUGHT MY ATTENTIONS
IN THE FIRST PLACE

LIKE NO
EXPECTATION/OBLIGATION,
BUT YOU ON MY COUCH
FEELS LIKE AN
INEVITABILITY

Fall
fell

a little too fast

into laps you left
me alone

falling faster
than leaves

from trees outside
inside voices & metaphors

for falling
out of love

the way you most
certainly

fell

this

Fall.

dreams, no fever.

No anxiety
Just indulgence

..because Google Maps tells me you're
exactly 200 kilometers away

and I'm nothing if not
wasted time and a full tank of gas.

SEEING YOU ON WEEKENDS IS SOMETHING
SEEING YOU ON ONE WEEKEND
MADE ME SPOILED TO.

SO I'M IN THIS RESTAURANT
HAVING SHOWN VACCINE
PASSPORTS

AND

APPROPRIATELY PHOTOGENIC
REPRESENTATIONS ON PHOTO ID

WHEN THE NEWS BREAKS
THAT ALL THIS IS OVER

AND

THE CAPACITY LIMITS WE'RE
COLLECTIVELY **OBEYING**/
IGNORING

CAN LOSE THE WORD BEFORE
/IGNORING,

*and I'm not

IGNORING

THE LOOK IN YOUR EYES

EYES THAT DON'T **MAKE SENSE**
AND YET

SOMEHOW,

WITH ANNOUNCEMENTS LIKE THE
ONE JUST ANNOUNCED

TELL US AT LEAST SOMETHING IS

STARTING TO.

fuck these masks

while they make those eyes
pop

those eyes that don't make
sense

they at least make the kind
of sense

that tells me

looking at the rest of that
resplendent little face

is better for quelling

the ocean of anxiety

that gazes back at me

from the table we wait to be
seated at

for the remainder of the
revealing.

feel like you're hours and hours worth of
conversation.

and exploration.

my list of amusing muses
aren't always amused
by the ones they figure
aren't about them;

and so you've got them all on their
collective toes

tipping
and
trying

to discern the length of
your pretty long
pretty little legs

and

you've got them collectively hoping
the height of their high ponys

collectively touches
the really high height of
your high fucking pony.

This one is fat
like your fat little ass

the way you barely fit
into those tights you barely fit
into

has me,
into you and

this fat little volume
that I'm about to finish

so you can be more to me
than the reason I picked up the pen

again

and to finish it.

petty as fuck
but you're here for it.

pretty as fuck
and I'm here for it.

COME OVER
AND LEAVE THE BAGGAGE
WHERE THE BAGGAGE IS BETTER OFF

BACK HOME AND WONDERING
WHERE THE LOVE OF HIS LIFE, TOO

UP AND RAN OFF TO

LOST LIKE THAT SOCK
FROM THE LAUNDRY YOU LEFT
HIM TO

TOO

ON YOUR WAY OUT THE DOOR
AND
MOTHERFUCKING

MORE THAN METAPHORICALLY.

LET'S BE HONEST
THAT MAN YOU WENT OFF
AND MARRIED
IS BETTER FOR 99 REASONS

99 REASONS AND THEY'RE
ALL
RIGHT

99 REASONS, SAVE
1

YOU'RE HERE RIGHT NOW
WITH ME

THE WAY YOU NEVER
REALLY
LEFT.

•••

WAIT, BEFORE YOU GET MAD
ABOUT THAT 99 REASONS
SHIT,

REMEMBER THE POEM ABOUT
THAT MAN YOU WENT OFF
AND MARRIED

COULD BE ABOUT YOU
OR
YOU
OR
YOU
OR
YOU
OR
YOU,

YOU ALL PREFER PATTERNS
AND,
DESPITE SAID 99 REASONS
I'M THE
1
YOU ALL HAVE IN COMMON,

COLD COMFORT FOR LOVING

THE LOST THINGS
YOU ALL SO COMMONLY
LOVE.

don't go

stay

don't go

stay

don't go

stay

don't go

stay

don't go

stay

i broke you
like that toy

you broke me
like that boy

i guess i never really stopped being

scared and too

and

entirely too afraid
to face up to

breaking the tiny pretty things

boys like me
always seem to break.

...

(late)

NOVEMBER.

FORGIVE ME
BUT FOR A GUY WHO SPENDS HIS FRIDAYS
GETTING PUNCHED IN THE FACE

IM HERE FOR ANY METAPHORICAL BEATINGS
YOU AND YOUR TOO RAPIDLY BEATING HEART
ARE ENTHUSIASTICALLY MOVING
RAPIDLY PARTING LIPS

TO MORE THAN METAPHORICALLY BEAT ME.

When working on it

isn't working out

I'm both viable option/inevitable
conclusion

wrapped up in one pretty, pretty much more
than a little self-destructive package.

After all of this
whining/introspection/self-
destruction/reflection/misery...

...it looks like there might be light at
the end of this proverbial tunnel,
pandemically (is that a word?) speaking,
so

bye.

www.ingramcontent.com/pod-product-compliance
Lightning Source LLC
Chambersburg PA
CBHW072153100526
44589CB00015B/2206
9781777019167